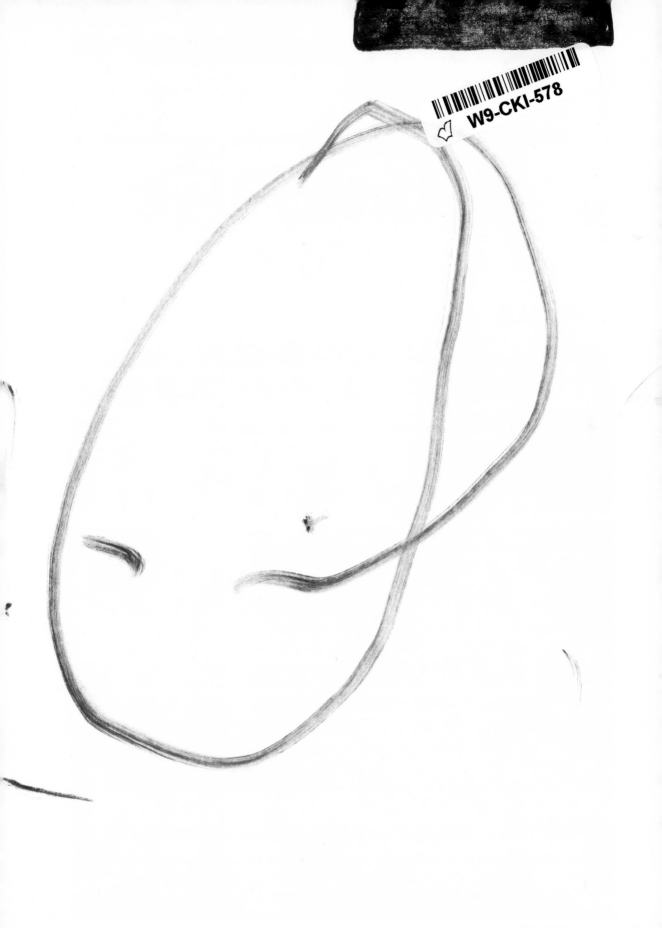

LEARN THE VALUE OF

Self Control

◆

by ELAINE P. GOLEY

Illustrated by Karen Park

◆

ROURKE ENTERPRISES, INC.
VERO BEACH, FL 32964

Library of Congress Cataloging-in-Publication Data

Goley, Elaine P., 1949–
    Learn the value of self control.

    Summary: Gives examples of self-control and demonstrates in two brief stories how it may be used in daily life.
    1. Self-control—Juvenile literature.
[1. Self-control]   I. Title.
BJ1533.D49G65   1989   179'.9   89-4530
ISBN 0-86592-397-3

Self Control

Do you know what **self control** is?

Having **self control** means being quiet when others are talking.

Self control is eating just one cookie between meals.

Not hitting your brother when you're angry
with him, is **self control.**

Self control is being quiet and listening when your teacher is speaking to the class.

Letting your sister choose the piece of pie
she wants before you take yours, is **self control.**

Self control is asking politely for something
you want instead of having a temper tantrum.

Being cheerful when your mom asks you to pick up your clothes, even if you feel grouchy, is **self control.**

14

Waiting until the teacher calls on you instead of shouting out the answer, is **self control.**

Self control is practicing your flute lessons before you go out to play.

Learning not to shout when your sister takes
your games, is **self control.**

Self control is waiting patiently in line to buy your movie ticket.

Waiting until Christmas to open your presents is **self control.**

Self control is letting your sister watch
her favorite TV show when you want to watch
something else.

Being polite when someone is rude,
is using **self control.**

Self control means being nice to someone
you don't like.

Doing your homework before you read your
favorite book, is using **self control.**

If you count to ten when you're angry instead
of shouting, that's **self control.**

Self Control

Jill had waited patiently for her birthday to come. Her mother hinted that one of her birthday presents would be a special surprise. Her mom baked a cake and invited some of Jill's friends to her birthday party.

Jill knew that her presents were in the hall closet. She wanted to open them to see what the special surprise was.

Instead, Jill helped her mother decorate the table with party favors and hats for her party.

How did Jill use **self control**?
How can you use **self control** at home?

Self Control

Donny was watching an interesting TV program about dinosaurs. They used realistic animation to show how dinosaurs walked, hunted prey, and fought with other dinosaurs. Donny's favorite subject was dinosaurs. He had dinosaur tee shirts, dinosaur models and a really neat dinosaur poster on his bedroom wall.

The TV program was really interesting. His teacher had asked the class to watch it.

Donny's sister, Sara, changed the channel. "I want to watch this movie," she said.

Donny was annoyed, but he said in a quiet voice: "My teacher wants me to watch this program." Then he changed the channel back to the dinosaur program.

How did Donny use **self control**?
How can you use **self control** at home?
At school?